THE TUMBLING BOX

ISBN 10: 0-9815010-4-4
ISBN 13: 978-0-9815010-4-8
LCCN: 2009930018

C&R Press
PO Box 4065
Chattanooga, TN 37405

www.crpress.org

THE TUMBLING BOX

Allison Funk

Acknowledgments

Grateful acknowledgment is made to the following journals in which these poems first appeared (sometimes in earlier versions or with different titles): *Cincinnati Review* ("The Escape Artist in Winter," "The Vanishing Lady Act," and "Notes on a Prairie: Late Summer"); *Court Green* ("The Escape Artist Performing the Straitjacket Release"); *Image* ("The Madonna with the Iris" and "Virgin and Child with a Dragonfly"); *Mid-American Review* ("Camera Obscura"); *Natural Bridge* ("Notes on a Prairie: Early Summer"); *New Letters* ("Singing Descant"); *New Orleans Review* ("The Holy Family with Three Hares"); *Orion* ("He Wouldn't Leave Me Alone—"); *Pleiades* ("After Saying He Was a Danger to Himself or Others"); *Poetry* ("The Escape Artist in an Underwater Casket"); *Poetry Review (U.K.)* ("Penelope at Home," "Boltonia," and "The Virgin with the Animals"); *Prairie Schooner* ("Rowing," "Flying West," "Shadow Play," and "As If Ovid Had Written Their Story"); *Shenandoah* ("The Tumbling Box," "An Entry in the Escape Artist's Diary," and "True Prairie").

"My Mother Would Be a Falconress" (excerpt of six lines) by Robert Duncan, from Bending the Bow, © 1968 by Robert Duncan. Reprinted by permission of New Directions Publishing Corp.

"*Ephemeroptera*" was commissioned by the Calouste Gulbenkian Foundation for the anthology *Wild Reckoning*, published in London in 2004.

I would like to thank poets Jennifer Atkinson, Cleopatra Mathis, Eric Pankey, Jason Sommer, and Jane O. Wayne for criticism that helped shape this book. Thanks to Southern Illinois University Edwardsville, which has generously supported my work. Gratitude to Stacey Lynn Brown, who introduced me to C&R Press, and to Ryan G. Van Cleave and Chad Prevost, its founders, for believing in this book. Appreciation to the Ragdale Foundation, Yaddo, and the Hawthornden Castle International Writers Retreat for providing me with space and quiet to write. My love to my parents for raising me in a house full of books and to George, whose patience and goodness I rely upon most.

Table of Contents

My mother would be a falconress,
and I her gerfalcon raised at her will,
from her wrist sent flying, as if I were her own
pride, as if her pride
knew no limits, as if her mind
sought in me flight beyond the horizon.

Robert Duncan

The Tumbling Box

As a child
I learned to keep my stories to myself.
Inside they spun

like stones in a tumbler,
one of those rotating drums
for polishing

amethyst, jasper, rose quartz
to the smoothness of a lozenge
on the tongue.

And so in conversations
I lagged behind.
When pressed to speak

I'd agree with someone else—
to more than that,
who'd want to listen?

Even now I'm drawn
to another's version
of the tale of a woman

who said nothing
but what she heard first
from others.

Her voice trailing
after, repeating.
For Echo

nothing could have been worse
than falling in love
with Narcissus.

Unless they'd had children.
To this familiar story
what can I add

that hasn't been said before?
Over and *over*,
my stones remind me.

Those untrustworthy masters!
Always reversing themselves,
turning toward me,

then away, upside, down.
Never letting me have the last word
with their never ending

end over end.
Is anybody listening?
End. Over. End.

Camera Obscura

Outside my dark chamber,
everyone, everything's moving

around a little lake in the middle of which
a fountain wells up. Too much? Water

issuing from water. The lake that jettisons itself,
then takes back what it had kept

below the surface, just to make its confession again.
The way the swings the children pump skyward

do, the way the teeter-totter argues—
this is what I will;

this what I return to.
Beyond: a gazebo pretending the cheer

of another century, freshly painted
a clotted cream. The red maple,

its courtesan, the only tree this late
leaved. A day warm enough to be summer,

a school bus passing, a woman
chasing her child to the edge—

safe, safe
the maple, the relentless fountain,

even (having just crossed the park)
my son

until through my lens he arrives,
capsized. The future,

who invited it in,
the future that inverts everything?

After Saying He Was a Danger to Himself or Others

They said he couldn't leave. No matter, then,
if he'd changed his mind. Wanted to go. Called
them motherfuckers, kicked, and punched the wall
in. It took four large men to tie him down.
Strangers with no memory of the dawn
he was born—from the unseen, his long fall
toward the light, his scream upon arrival—
or the years between Brigham and the room
in this hospital where they have sent her
to wait. Once he is bound, the orderlies
move him on a stretcher from the ER,
take him to a locked ward on the fifth floor.
They tell her to leave. It doesn't matter
to anyone that she is his mother.

Watermarks

She first knew terror
when he couldn't breathe.
Not him, amen, she repeated,
holding her fevered infant close
until steam opened his lungs.

~

A watermark. The scar
that barely shows through vellum
when a page is held to light.

It was hard to see at first.

Like a fever
though not one you can measure
or cure.

By his adolescence, anyone could see
how ravaged she'd become trying.

~

Later she wanted to disappear
like the see-through creatures
she'd heard of.

Hardly a mark on the phantom octopus,

glass catfish—spirits
that barely ripple the water
when they pass.

Dot of retina, heart a spot.

She'd be nobody
you could find. Shadow-free.

~

Bud that should have grown,

blossomed like the magnolia,
plum-pink
brushed over a pale wash,

should have blown like that petal
when the wind carries it down,
turns it up on the river,

should have become
a little boat.

~

Sing the mark—
one, quarter one, half one,
quarter less twain. The water's
still too low. How can she move?
Hull scraping bottom. Bottomed out.

~

When her son told her strangers
beat on his walls,
sounds began to register
on her skin.

Her husband's footsteps on the stairs
(which never bothered her before).

Words too—
a tingling in her feet (*run*),
numbing of the hands (*stay*).
Mother made her squeamish.
The ping of a voice
could jolt her crazy bone.

Lock me up, she wished,
before I feel everything I hear.

Or soothe me
with a waterfall's tone
upon tone.

~

If she can't detect the wavelengths
birds can with their extra cone
tuned to ultraviolet light

(one cardinal through the eyes
of another—not blood—
reddish-blue)

she could be blind to what's visible
to her son.

All the predators and prey,
bruised.

~

On the oval table she's inherited:
a white watermark where someone left a glass.

Denatured alcohol should remove it.
With a small amount on a cloth,
rub to lighten the ring.

But what will work on the scorch scar,
half circle, darker
than the muddy mahogany?

Permanent, the initials
a child has carved in the grain.

~

At flood stage
the stilts a house is built upon
disappear, the river slips
under the front door.

~

She marks the distance as she swims.
Twenty-five yards. One lap, back.

This is no map, no get-away route
to the lavender fields of France.

Half a mile and she's gone
nowhere. At the shallow end
she grips the lip of the pool
and kicks, furiously, in place.

Then takes a breath
and starts down the lane again
to strengthen her heart.

An Entry in the Escape Artist's Diary

Yes. Willingly bound.
The lights dimmed to gloaming,

evening, the eventual, medieval
dark. So far back

who can remember the first knot—
whatever we called it—

salt or sweet on the tongue,
the story of the body slack,

then tightening? Or another:
love confused with labor,

the breath a tangle—
half hitch, long splice, noose.

Now, while I try to slip the knots,
mimicking the wind's contortions,

whose cry, what bell almost beyond hearing?
Beyond seeing, the little boat I'm in

drifting free of its moorings.
As if under a scarf,

lake, mountains, everything loved
is vanishing?

Boltonia

It's a fugitive species,
the botanist explains
as she leads me into a mob of willows,

giant ragweed and cheatgrass.
Just beyond us, on a river
cramped by its levees and dammed,

a lock lifts a barge with the care
I took to comfort my newborn
and lay him back down to sleep.

By another river, a mother,
knowing his end if she kept him,
released her son in a basket

woven of rushes, a story
not unlike the one my friend tells of seeds
riding the backs of annual floods

before the Illinois was reined in.
Today we've come out to a parched plain
to look for survivors.

What they need is that first world
we've lost, she says.
So late in August,

how can I hope to find
Boltonia decurrens
head high with frosty-pink blooms?

Or my endangered one
whom I'm pursuing too
in this bottomland.

Sesame

Open, sesame,
    a child's ear hears.
Seed small as the mustard's

    said to grow and grow
until the birds of the air
    come to nest in its branches.

Seed small as the one we start from.

    Far from here
a young boy asks his mother
    to read him a story.

And though night has shuttered the windows—
    the room they're in, bureau,
clothes going slowly out of focus—

    the lamp above them makes a full moon
on the first page of their book.
    A milky pool.

And they go in, into their story
    as if it were a cave filled with gold.
They go in like thieves.

            ~

    There was once a young man
who dreamed of murderous thieves
    lurking just outside his door.

Inside, in a space as cramped
     and bleak as a cave,
nights passed, and days,

     often without his notice.
(Gunshots turned up so high,
     the blinds pulled down all the way.)

Next to his bed he kept a sharp stick
     he never wanted to use,
but wouldn't it be crazy,

     he thought,
to have no protection?
     Crazier still to go out

where anyone
     could be waiting.
Even if he'd wanted to,

     after all this time
he'd forgotten the words
     he would need there.

As if his mouth,
     like the door on its hinges,
was locked.

                    ~

     Afraid of losing him,
I remind my son of Scheherazade,
     how she survived,

thanks to her stories.
    And so the hard nights pass,
I tell my grown son.

    I have no stories of my own,
he says with his eyes.
    Every one you have stolen.

~

Water, oxygen, go in.
    Wake the sesame
in its shallow bed of silt

    and do not leave
until it begins to root
    like an animal rummaging

for what it needs,
    becoming stem, leaf
pale flower,

    pods that snap open
at last—
    spilling their tear-shaped seeds.

~

Amen.

    Though, of course, the next night
the story begins again.
    The thieves—

where were they hiding?
   the young boy asks his mother
who's reading Ali Baba's story to him.

   A servant found those
plotting to kill her master
   in jars, she says

with an arm encircling her son.
   After she'd disposed of them
Marjana turned to their captain,

   who sat at Ali Baba's table
swallowing his unsalted meat.
   Girded with a silver belt and masked,

she performed a dance with a dagger,
   thrusting it forward and drawing it back,
as if to stab someone else,

   then herself. Forward and back,
faster and faster until in the blur
   no one knew who

was the most endangered,
   master, servant, or thief.
Had we been there ourselves,

   says the boy's mother
as she turns out the light,
   we could not have told them apart.

True Prairie

Behind the shadow a word is,
another always waits,
the way "false" followed me this morning
as I walked through a prairie called "true,"

remembering false foxglove,
downy false foxglove, smooth.
Most wildflowers have at least one counterfeit.
Even Solomon's seal,

though most of us couldn't tell false
from true apart
unless we broke the impostor off
at the stem to find a circular scar

rather than Solomon's signet:
two interlocked triangles inside a ring.
How easily we're confused,
we who lack the king's wisdom.

Poets may be the worst—
or mothers—
always failing true-false tests.
Distracted by resemblances.

For example, the tall grasses I'd known
yesterday by their plum-purple stems
this morning, dew-covered,
looked sheathed in ice—a hoarfrost—

turning the season I was in
into another one.
Making summer false.
False August.

Precipitous winter, coming too early,
coming to claim the child, cut
the living in half.
I am at the mercy of my seasons.

The premonition I shall wake
to find my son dead in my arms
if I can't tell the true mother
from the one holding on.

He Wouldn't Leave Me Alone—

the bird with the faded look
of secondhand clothes.
Over and over from the juniper bush
he lifted off—then crashed:
the flash of his beak
detonating against glass.
After which he fell to the ground,
then hopped back up to the branch
to face me again—
each time at the same pane
of the glassed-in porch
where I was writing.
As if he were a wind-up.
Had some mechanism inside
he couldn't turn off.
One day. The next.
Whenever I looked up
from my desk, he looked back
like a fledgling,
although fully grown,
repeating branch, glass, grass, branch
until I mimed back
as if to my own child—*fly*.

Virgin and Child with a Monkey

After an engraving by Albrecht Dürer (about 1498)

Where has the monkey come from?
    The last thing she'd imagine
Among the irises, the lilies of the valley
    That fill a German garden.
But she welcomes the creature,
    Loves how he wriggles his cute little nose,
Climbs up into her lap to comb his fingers
    Through her hair, playing
Just like a child. Sweet thing, she calls him
    Before she begins to tire of his chattering.
So much noise, how can a person think?
    Try, she tries, but cannot quiet him.
And finding no way out
    Of the walled garden they're in,
She begins to despair,
    Looking for a shady section
As far as possible from the commotion.
    Everywhere she hides now she hears
His raving, yes, it sounds like raving,
    And her son, poor baby,
Days she cannot tell them apart,
    One greedy as the next, their babbling
Driving her to distraction, to question
    Even her own sense—
Soon the monkey's tail
    Will snake everywhere in her garden,
She'll see nothing else.

The Escape Artist Performing the Straitjacket Release

Slipping out of the jacket
isn't the trick.

It's getting free of what coils around me
daytime and night. A boa

of dread worse than the straps
tightening across my chest,

constricting my arms. It's easy to cry,
The insane can't escape what I can

when like a monarch from its cocoon
I emerge to the amazement of all.

But at home in my winding sheet, wrapped
and spinning, I'm pinioned again,

the taste of buckles
and straps on my tongue.

As If Ovid Had Written Their Story

There was a *before*,
though he could not have known
    the girl she was once:

adrift, nearly weightless—
    pollen, or a sixteenth note
gone as soon as it sounds.

    She says, Darling,
and he hears her growl.
    She comes closer,

and he takes his aim,
    seeing talons and fangs.
And who is he, if not a changeling?

    Where's his damp crown
the dusk of wild mushrooms
    unearthed from the loam?

Grown, the smallest rustling
    disturbs him, turns her,
nearly everyone, into a predator.

    In the wind starting up now
she'd like to run from her son,
    but in the dim woods

she can't see beyond,
    she is held
by what's held against her.

The Virgin with the Animals

*After a work by Albrecht Dürer with pen and ink and watercolor on
paper (about 1503)*

Tsk, tsk, chides the bird by the carnations,
   Bird the hue of ripe blueberries,
And almost that small. Beautiful,
   Her garden seen by anyone else,
But the woman's too busy blaming herself
   To notice the rosy peonies,
Three blooms on the iris.
   In her head all the animals
Are talking at once—
   Not only the parrot on the post
Repeating her every fear for her son—
   The stag beetle, the crab,
The swan family in the stream
   Know this is no Eden,
Much as it looks like the childhood
   We want for our children.
Still, I'd like to be convinced.
   I listen to the prayer
The water's repeating,
   I want to believe.
But I begin to hear the animals, too,
   The dog that will guard the boy
As he grows up senses they'll come—
   Like the fox in the foreground,
The men who'll arrest him.
   Then who will save him?
Asks the horned owl
   Inside the stump. And the woman
Who has no say in this matter
   Falls dumb.

Lock and Key

The bars through which she speaks to her son—
even these become hers to escape from.
The voice inside her beginning:
a sharp blow, keyhole down,
easily opens the spring: that voice
always calling, coming
with its accompanying visions—
her very own serpent in the garden
hissing *Free him.*
But what if, this time, she chose
not to listen? For once,
lay down the key she carried
under her layers of clothing
and walked out like a god herself
into the cool afternoon.

The Holy Family with Three Hares

After a woodcut by Albrecht Dürer (about 1497-8)

It's an old story.
   Yet the artist returns with his knives
Sharpened to carve the folds
   Of the gown, the child
In his mother's arms.
   Like the little hare and its mother
At her feet, Mary and her boy
   Overlap. They could be one body,
Much as the tree in the distance
   Is forked. The pages
In the book the child is holding
   Are bound. Can't she guess
How their story will end?
   No mother's intuition?
The third hare, on its way out
   Of the picture when Dürer catches it
Mid-flight, senses something.
   The small birds, too,
Winging east and west. Even Joseph,
   Walking stick in his right hand,
Hat and cloak in the left.
   But Mary, doting on her son,
Misses the angels we can see
   Suspended above her
Bearing the crushing weight of a crown.
   By the time the child turns the page,
Hares, father, will have flown.
   Another page turned
And the son, determined to die,
   Is gone.
But what of the page Dürer hasn't given us,

The mother afterwards?
After the rending
  And weeping, *shiva*,
Yahrzeit, amen and again amen,
  After the rains of winter, the winds?
That we must imagine
  For ourselves.

Gothic Maidens

After a series of prints titled "Gothic Maidens" by Georg Baselitz

One would extend her arm if she could.

Another flex her ungainly foot.

It's what they've become—arms. Aching feet. Buttocks. Breasts.

The cleft we come from.

So little space—eleven by seven, the inches allotted to each.

All faceless. Defaced?

Dark, thin—what's left of them. I think of barbed wire.

Did they fence themselves in?

Once I rented a room to escape. Went there days to be alone. But I found it too big for just me. So I made a room within a room of bricks and shelves, lined the four sides with books. Locked myself up.

And so each of us lives within herself.

Like stacking wooden dolls. Each smaller than the next.

A dream within a dream within the dreamed.

Shutting up like a telescope.

It was November. Then December. By New Year's I'd dismantled my shelves. Carried every one of my fifty bricks back down a long flight of stairs. Locked the door. Moved out.

What's inside? one of the maidens might ask if she had a voice. *What's out?*

Inside out?

I wish I had an answer—but I'm topsy-turvy as they are, wedged upside down in their womb-size rooms.

I remember when young I traveled easily over borders. Italy, England, France. At each, an official took my passport, let me in, let me out when I wanted to leave.

Except where West Germany met East. Suddenly afraid, I looked through an electric fence in the rain to the other side: dogs, searchlights, guards. Baselitz's naked women seem to remember this. And worse.

Now I worry the boxes they're in are coffins.

And the flowers a few have—were they left for the dead?

Oh, let them be at least as lifelike as the virgins on the portals of medieval cathedrals. Each in her niche.

Some wise, others foolish.

Every one learning how to keep her lamp lit.

Shadow Play

The world. Our sun. And the moon.
    Not a family exactly,
        though some call the first

Mother Earth.
    And the three can be seen
        to be familial in the way they circle

one another—the moon
    leashed to its mother,
        mother lassoed herself—

the tethers invisible
    but felt on nights like this
        when our brimming satellite,

sun, world are all in alignment.
    A moment, we might say,
        of accord,

or a model instead
    of how some of us come
        to shadow each other.

Like when my wooden ball landed
    between my son's and a wicket.
        At ten he swung his mallet

to knock my globe sky high—
    out of the game,
        yard, block, beyond

the reach of glistening grass,
  straight out of the universe.
   Child's play,

as onto a cotton screen
  the shadows of puppets are cast.
   The figure that grows

and grows until its adversary
  is overwhelmed,
   much as the umbral dusk

of the earth seeps, then floods
  over the moon,
   the moon over our house,

a curtain drawn,
  then opening again
   on another act.

Penelope at Home

At first light she imagines crimson,
threads stained with saffron,
the madder root's orange.

But what use if the wool's not
between her forefinger and thumb—and,
and, this is it: how can she bear to begin,

start over each morning,
when it's all she can do to dress?
The food she puts in her mouth,

tasteless. The least wind
has subsided, she says to herself
as a sailor might to his ship.

How can *she* move it?
The body that through childhood and since
had borne her, always headed somewhere

as if possessed of a power
outside her. Anymore,
to go on, she forces the voices

down, one after the next
calling from inside her house.
Loudest: her son blaming her

for his father's absence
until she escapes to her loom
where armed with her *spatha*,

the one sword she owns,
she tightens the weave
to keep him, everything out.

At noon, she vows
to have the last word,
but who knows when she'll finish

her pattern of doubled hearts?
Each lobe coiled like the sea snail
prized for its drop of blue purple.

Torchlight shows her unraveling,
how at night she tugs, she tears out
the strands of her hair.

Dark and graying they fall
as slowly as motes to the floor
where the threads she wove by day,

now unstrung, also lie—
one over, one under the other.
Undone!

the chorus of a hundred mollusks
sacrificed for their tint
cry out from the fringes,

undone.
A shroud, she'd lied
when asked at first,

not guessing it would come to this:
every day she rises
to weave herself one.

When the Left Hand Isn't Playing

it must surely be listening to the other
that is.

Hovering above the keyboard,
it's poised as if over a loved one,
watchful, protective, afraid even

of what
it does not say.

But the woman in the second row,
center, thinks she understands—

alone, the right hand is playing
Beethoven with such abandon,
she feels at the edge of something

herself, something even the conductor
moving his baton on the other shore,
the far side of the Steinway,

cannot control,
something like a thermal
that the quiet one, the bird-hand
seems to be riding,

though not for long.

Stricken: a flag on a pole beaten about by the wind;
stiffening, a hand held above the heart
to keep from overflowing a wound.

All this time the right hand continues,
con brio, oblivious
of what the left one seems, eloquently,
to be signing.

He's of two minds,
she says to herself, the woman in seat 105
who empathizes with the pianist
(a word she keeps rearranging into *pain*).

Even here in this concert hall
where she's come for music,

the current running against the pulse
argues for silence,

that emptiness below middle C.

So let it end, thinks the woman

just before the largo begins.
Finally: the left hand joins the right
in favor of serenity,

another key, the island of E major,
or some place more remote still—

where, dazed,
she could travel forever
the tributaries of air.

The Vanishing Lady Act

She knows dozens of variations,
though most often she's an ordinary woman,
any one selected from the audience

by the magician who passes her the cup
or waves a vial under her nose,
from which she falls into the deep sleep

she's in when she's dreaming.
The few props necessary for her trick:
the chair in which she sits and the trap door under it,

which no one can see.
In a moment, she'll be gone—nothing left
but a handkerchief, the lace a wave leaves

when it withdraws from a beach.
Where is she then?
Even she's not certain where she's traveling

undercover: hurricane, hail,
cloudburst, drizzle, oh the relief
of being a single drop or less

until—so habitual it seems unwilled—
she's seated in the audience again,
saying *Here I am.*

The Escape Artist in Winter

I'm under it again, that foot of ice.
No headroom. On me, the weight of a house.

This winter's hard as the year the river froze over,
that December they bore a hole

the size fishermen cut for their bait,
then lowered me down, bound hands and feet.

Wouldn't you think I'd free myself fast,
seeing through the lens just above me

the faces I'd left?
But I'd imagined death as a spaciousness

I hadn't known on earth, another element—
not water exactly or air.

I wanted to float there. The spirit, though—
it lists toward the light, poor trapped one

with me under a layer of ice. For her
I fought the current sucking at me like a child,

all the time wanting to open my mouth,
wanting to drink, swallow the murky liquid I was in.

But I chewed at my bindings instead,
remembered how to breathe without air,

and we swam toward the surface
she and I, as if finned,

as if there were a school of us.
We were a multitude.

The Madonna with the Iris

*After an oil painting on lime by Albrecht Dürer's workshop
(about 1500-10)*

As usual, she's enclosed in a garden—
   Always a wall,
Stone or wattle, around her.
   The wall is the body,
The garden the soul, some believe,
   Though not the woman inside,
Who dwells on the life
   Shut in and shut out. Beyond—
What artists term background—
   She calls *before*.
Sometimes it's the Magi on their way
   To the birth. Or shepherds
Guarding their flocks.
   But she remembers further back,
Before the child stirred within her,
   The hills she fled to
When she wanted to be alone.
   Here, in the painting,
The one his assistants will finish,
   Dürer doesn't try to imagine her past,
But knowing what's ahead for her,
   And having a heart,
He's made an opening
   In the half-ruined wall beyond the iris,
The plantains and dandelions,
   Beyond the turf-covered bench
Where she sits with her child,
   An arch through which
She can find, unbroken,
   The level line of the sea.

Turner's Yellow

In "The Burning of the Houses of Lords and Commons"
  J.M.W. Turner may as well have dipped his brush
    in the flames racing across a prairie's acres,
      his canvas gives off that much heat,

the same sulfurous haze blurring,
  scumbling my Midwest, his Thames,
    the blaze that starts, the wind that carries it
      until everything's molten

on the artist's brush, the fire runs away
  from the torch that set it.
    Turner's yellow. Is it any wonder
      the artist tried to rein it in,

taming it to gild a river's surface,
  then turning it bronze as the sun
    seen through mist?
      Bridge, tower, he must have said,

as if to keep from disappearing
  what he could still recognize
    through the smoke surrounding the boat
      from which he watched Parliament burn.

Witness. As he claimed he was later
  aboard another ship, in a blizzard so fierce he knew
    he'd be swept away if not lashed to the mast.
      Four hours he was bound, he said,

not expecting to live, but determined to record it if he did.
What? Not wind exactly or waves.
Not only the jaundiced light about to be snuffed out,
says his brush. Hostage to no form,

what rages at gale force held him.
But longing to make a home for it
in the visible world, Turner called his painting
"Snow Storm—Steam-Boat off a Harbour's Mouth

making Signals in Shallow Water,
and going by the Lead.
The Author was in this Storm on the Night
the Ariel left Harwich."

Thinking of Goethe's color wheel,
the sun that's a fireball,
I imagine how Turner must have begun
a painting—needing like me

to burn away what grows up
unwanted, weedy, making it harder
and harder to see the horizon.
With the idea of starting over

I begin as if I were lighting a backfire
that's slow to catch, downwind,
thinking creek, bluff, road, ditch,
careful to contain the burn.

At this point wouldn't Turner
still be hearing the carriages
outside his studio windows? A theater
of vendors, clocks striking the hour,

then critics, children
    he'd prefer not to remember,
        the racket getting louder, then harsher—
        who can bear it he thinks—

until the wind shifts
    and the Author's alone with a canvas,
        his landscape, nothing to stop
        the headfire blazing within.

Notes on a Prairie: Early Summer

Notice how the wildflowers open as if nothing restrains them.
No sign of a lock that's been picked, handcuffs sprung.

Coneflower, bee balm, sweet clover. Who can tell
how far they tunneled, if they fumbled like the blind

for a key? Dirt clings to none. None of them reeks
of the grave. Not the feathery pink showoff, queen-of-the-prairie,

or the towering cow parsnip that accepts whatever lands
in its nets. Even the loosestrife whose name betrays

a second self, the double life the blooms in the prairie conceal,
puts on purple as leisurely as a woman might draw a dark stocking

up over her ankle and knee, feeling the silkiness,
every inch of it, going on.

The woman I'm thinking of doesn't rush.
With the same ease, when it's time, she'll take it off.

The Escape Artist in an Underwater Casket

What was I thinking before the storm
brewing in my lungs began,

the sealed box I'm in sank to pool bottom?
Gone. The before

and before the before.
An hour down, my mind's a dizzy freight

I have to stop, so little oxygen,
got to find a rhythm,

inhale less to make it last.
The fact is between breaths

every minute's a test—
the voice a miner fears in the shaft,

the ghost in the coal dust
whispering promises

until I ring the bell to say more
air,

and I'm hauled to the surface,
blue newborn.

Ephemeroptera

Blizzard. Smoke. Interstellar
dust. Even my brother, the entomologist,
turns to metaphor,

awed by their emergence
over water. So thick
at times he covers his face

to keep from breathing them in.
Pale evening dun,
morning spinner.

How many dawns ago,
numberless dusks?
Call it

what astronomers do—
that past whose light
just now reaches us:

look-back time. His
and mine—our own becoming,
born of the milky ways

of love. Fragile once
as the earliest larva,
instar.

And later—in a house looking out
into a woods of tulip poplar,
rhododendron, down over train tracks

to a creek named Red Clay
where, in another eon,
fish swam before men

put out the lights of mayflies
smaller than the thumb
of the boy with a net

he was then.
Twenty-nine-o-one,
our address as children blurring

with the thousand-some species
of *Ephemeroptera*,
with prehistory, fossil time,

the millions of years mayflies
thrived in Permian streams,
Triassic, Jurassic,

feeding on infinitesimal diatoms
before vanishing
from our fouled creek.

It's another century
and we've been gone
from home as long as it's taken

them to return one by one
to their underworld
of silt and mud.

Some clinging to stones
in swift currents, others
hiding in gaps. With oar-like gills

the unbleached nymph
rows for dear oxygen,
spending years in between-time

molting over and over again—
all for as much as a single evening
when this wisp

growing not toward death
but into something
like the passions that consume us,

filamentous, breaks the water's surface
with crumpled wings
and, fast as a sleight of hand,

changes shape a final time
to become the luminous, meteoric
imago,

in whose likeness
may I recognize in what passes
what lasts.

Singing Descant

She hadn't always been an alto.
As a girl she'd even sung descant,
that high soprano line—
tinsel strung above the melody of a song,

a frill the weight of spindrift
or a Scottish *haar*, that mist
that vexes fishermen before it burns away.
Sea-fret, it's called on another coast,

which returns me to music
and the girl I find high above C
sharping a phrase with the tensile strength
of floss, a single filament

freighted with dew. And if I,
drawing it out, spinning it further,
were to assign this nearly sheer
counterpoint color, I'd venture

the pewter of hoarfrost or rime,
December's overcast reflected in ice,
even *glint* or *glitter*
(to account for a trace of gold).

She'd thought of her life then
as a part to be sung—
not a faultline ready to open—
and I won't have it, I won't

have her recall how often since
all seemed broken—not tonight,
not on this night clear as the Christmas
in which she was carried away

by her "round yon virgins,"
filling, then brimming
with her own light, the girl
in the magnitude of happiness

rendering the woman she would become
infinitesimal.

Els Caragols

in Catalonia

Nationalists and Republicans
    stopped people on afternoons like this.
        Shot them in front of their companions,

Nela said, as we walked by the river
    that cuts Lleida in half. Many
        caught in the middle of a kiss,

bending over to tie a daughter's shoe.
    Right here, along the Segre I'd crossed
        so often, pausing to look down

to stony bottom. Now,
    without warning, I was falling.
        Nothing left of my friend, mothers, old men,

but a liquid shimmering.
    A trick of the light on hot asphalt,
        wasn't it? But also how

I'd always thought it would happen—
    words, sense breaking up, foreign
        what I heard now from afar,

like the music that haunts me sometimes
    before waking. Owl, dove? No bird
        I ever recognize in the halftones

of dreaming, the dimly lit familiar
    described by those who've blacked out
        and come to or those who come back blinking

with jump-started hearts, the nearly gone.
     The woebegone sometimes too. How long
          had I been standing by the river thinking

of dying before, bleary-eyed, I saw
     a flickering? Like a candle
          about to be snuffed out by the wind,

then, focusing, sunlit grass.
     Every stream-green blade unfurled.
          But what was strung along the head high stalks?

Hundreds of them! One linked to the next
     like an add-a-pearl necklace.
          Caragols, insisted a voice I knew.

Nela, laughing. They're just *caragols*.
     And it was comical—confusing
          a common snail for a jewel.

But nothing seemed too small to notice then,
     least of all the life inside a labyrinth,
          its own miniature spiraling path.

Mira

Claustre, claustro, cloître. Any language can wall me in,
but inside a hilltop cloister rimmed by the chapels
of Our Lady of Succor and Eleven Thousand Virgins,
I found myself saying, savoring the beautiful Catalan word
for looking when through the petals of a tracery's lace
I looked out to the city below—

Lleida's avenues, shops, parks and churches
suddenly offering up their names.
Then on to the river Segre and across on *Pont Nou,*
thinking of the sea, beginning to see farther
as if one of the city's storks were leading me,
a woman in black grieving her own dead ends,

over the roofs, roads, and beyond
to the groves of apricots, olives, peaches,
and the creamy-pink blossoms soon to become
the sweet kernels of the almond I could almost taste
by traveling to where the longing
for *ametlla dolça* begins on the tongue.

Rowing

Each time he twists to look
    over his shoulder, the boat
        follows, veering off course.

When rowing it's best
    to face where you've been,
        not where you're going,

I venture, knowing, as elsewhere,
    my son fears he'll be overtaken
        as soon as his back is turned.

Slaps on the water's surface
    his only response,
        I say nothing more for now,

anxious to avoid the usual exchanges
    that capsize us both.
        But in this sturdy aluminum rowboat

on our first family outing in years,
    the sky brightening, the island
        we're headed for coming into sight,

we're suddenly finding the right words
    as if they'd been waiting—
        a lake full, all we have to do is cast.

He's even talking to my husband,
    my husband to him, and in minutes
        everything joins in the conversation—

the bailer clanging like a cowbell,
   twin oarlocks answering the crickets
      on shore—an improbable chorus

cheering him on
   as my son rows us across the lake,
      lifting the oars and lowering them

with such ease
   they seem to catch the mercurial water,
      and, as lightly, release it.

Notes on a Prairie: Late Summer

The tall grass is flattened where the deer bedded down.
In the morning it shines like the new fawn its mother's licked clean.

The prairie they've disappeared into is waking up also.
Still, little moves but my shadow along the mown path

and the poplar's leaves busy as waves turning over—
silver, then dark green again.

Later the wind will rise, making the whole field look tidal,
making everything living bow down: the Joe Pye weed,

queen-of-the-prairie, the coneflowers locals call Lazy Susans.
Already the bluestem taller than I am sways a little on its stalks,

the Indian grass nods south, then north. Heavy laden.
Believe it—pollen can blow anywhere,

though it's likely to stay close to home,
where it started, start again.

Virgin and Child with a Dragonfly

After an engraving by Albrecht Dürer (about 1495)

She doesn't notice it
　And neither do I
Until something starts up in us—
　Then suddenly: bronze
Between see-through wings,
　The dragonfly flashes its wand.
How ever, she wonders,
　Could she have missed
Its look-at-me look next to her hem?
　So much else to attend to, of course.
Joseph, what does he want,
　Arm slung over the back of her bench?
And the dear child himself
　With his little hand at her neck.
Once she's glanced away from them, though,
　She sees it *is* paradise. One, two, three,
More goldfinches flushed from the grass.
　And like a child now herself,
She claps others from hiding:
　Surprise! A monarch
Unfolds its fan; the live coal
　Of a cardinal glows.
Then just for fun (*red, red, another one*)
　She thinks how like the sour cherry
Ripening the bird is when it flies.
　And her mind, freed, flying now,
Sees from the stones the cardinal drops
　Each branch of a new tree flare.
Tinder, everything's tinder
　For the dragonfly's wick, she cries
Before she goes up, goes out.

Flying West

Crossing a continent she looks out
at the night behind, light ahead,

from under a door it seems.
The woman's reminded of the levees

back home, the flood waters rising,
how the vestige of day

will go under. For now, though,
she returns to the novel she's reading,

in which a body is floating downstream—
feast of crows and fish,

it hardly looks human.
She starts to make up a back-story

for the drowned—the man
had a troubled son, she imagines,

then, recognizing her own plot
in the one she's inventing,

stops. Oh, to be borne,
borne away, she almost says

out loud, knowing
she can keep the bloated face

of the moon behind her
only while aloft.

Still, she thinks,
neither there nor elsewhere yet,

she's free
as one crossing a tightrope can be.

Notes

The book's epigraph is an excerpt from Robert Duncan's poem "My Mother Would Be a Falconress" in *Bending the Bow* (New Directions, 1968).

"Sesame": Husain Haddawy's translation of "The Story of Ali Baba and the Forty Thieves" in *The Arabian Nights II* (W.W. Norton, 1995) was a resource during the writing of this poem.

"True Prairie": The tallgrass prairie in Illinois is sometimes called "the true prairie."

"Virgin and Child with a Monkey": For this poem and the others in the manuscript that refer to works by Albrecht Dürer, I use the artist's titles to title my poems.

"As If Ovid Had Written Their Story": Ovid's story of Callisto and Arcas, from his *Metamorphoses*, inspired this poem. I am indebted to the translation by Ted Hughes, *Tales of Ovid* (Farrar, Straus, Giroux, 1997).

"The Holy Family with Three Hares": In Jewish practice, *shiva* is a weeklong period of mourning after a family member's death. Annually, a family observes the deceased's *yahrzeit* (anniversary of the death).

"Gothic Maidens": Georg Baselitz's series of prints titled *Gothic Maidens* are in the collection of the Tate Modern Museum in London.

"The Escape Artist in Winter": My reading of Muriel Rukeyser's *Houdini: A Musical*, Act I, Scene 4 (Paris Press, 2002) prompted this poem.

"*Ephemeroptera*": The order of insects called *Ephemeroptera* includes mayflies. In their final adult form, mayflies mate and die in less than a day. This poem is dedicated to my brother David.

"*Els Caragols*": The setting for this poem is Lleida, in Catalonia (Spain), where many lives were lost during the Spanish Civil War. The city is well-known for its edible snails, called *els caragols* in Catalan.

"*Mira*": The cloister referred to is in *La Seu Vella* ("The Old See" or "Seat"), a Romanesque Gothic cathedral on a hill overlooking Lleida, in Catalonia. The imperative "*mira*" means "look" in Catalan.

"Flying West": The poem refers to an image of a body floating downstream from Jon Clinch's novel, *Finn* (Random House, 2007).